JR. GRAPHIC GHOST STORIES

THE WHITE LADY GHOST

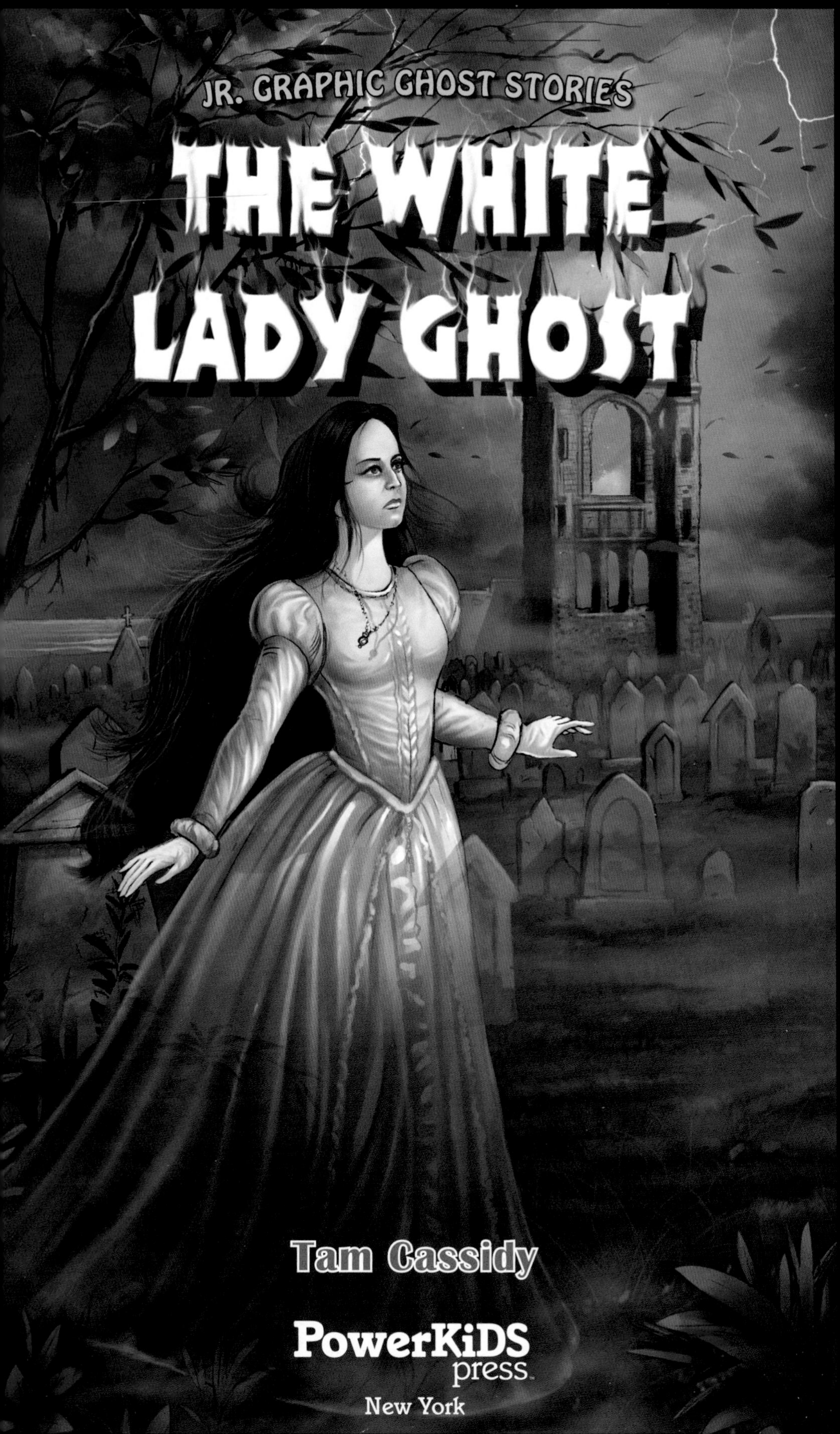

Tam Cassidy

PowerKiDS press

New York

Published in 2015 by The Rosen Publishing Group, Inc.
29 East 21st Street, New York, NY 10010

First Edition

Editor: Joanne Randolph
Book Design: Contentra Technologies
Illustrations: Contentra Technologies

Publisher's Cataloging Data

Cassidy, Tam.
The White Lady Ghost / by Tam Cassidy — first edition.
p. cm. — (Jr. graphic ghost stories)
Includes index.
ISBN 978-1-4777-7125-9 (library binding) — ISBN 978-1-4777-7126-6 (pbk.) — ISBN 978-1-4777-7127-3 (6-pack)
1. Ghosts — Juvenile literature. 2. Folklore — Juvenile literature. I. Title.
BF1461.C37 2015
398—d23

Manufactured in the United States of America

CPSIA Compliance Information: Batch #WS14PK2: For Further Information contact Rosen Publishing, New York, New York at 1-800-237-9932

Contents

Introduction

White Lady ghosts have appeared to people around the world. Usually, **observers** report that these spooky women are wearing white or pale gray dresses, but sometimes they are **clad** in other colors. Some White Lady ghosts are said to be mean or **vengeful**, but others seem quite gentle. Often these ghosts are linked to stories of tragedy or loss.

Main Characters

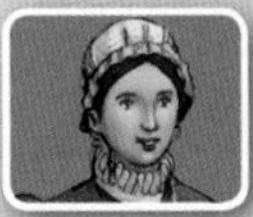

Mary, Queen of Scots (1542–1587) Also known as Mary Stuart, this Scottish queen led a dramatic life. Accused of plotting against her cousin Queen Elizabeth I of England, Mary was convicted of **treason** and beheaded.

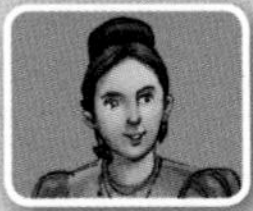

Mary Seaton (15?–15?) A **lady-in-waiting** to Mary, Queen of Scots, Mary Seaton (also spelled Seton) was one of the queen's companions. She was at Mary's side when the queen was executed. Tales of the White Lady of St. Andrews are based on her life.

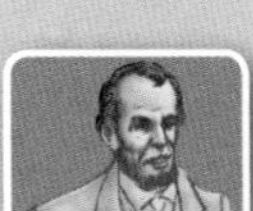

Abraham Lincoln (1809–1865) Sixteenth president of the United States. He served as president from 1861 until 1865.

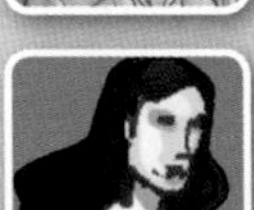

Patricia Wilson (?) A guest who died in the Seelbach Hotel, in Louisville, Kentucky.

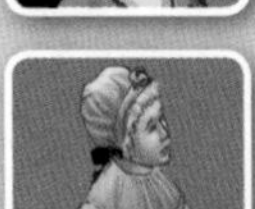

Abigail Adams (1744–1818) The wife of President John Adams, who served as president from 1797 to 1801.

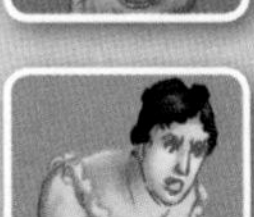

Dolley Madison (1768–1849) The wife of President James Madison, who served as president from 1809 to 1817.

The White Lady Ghost

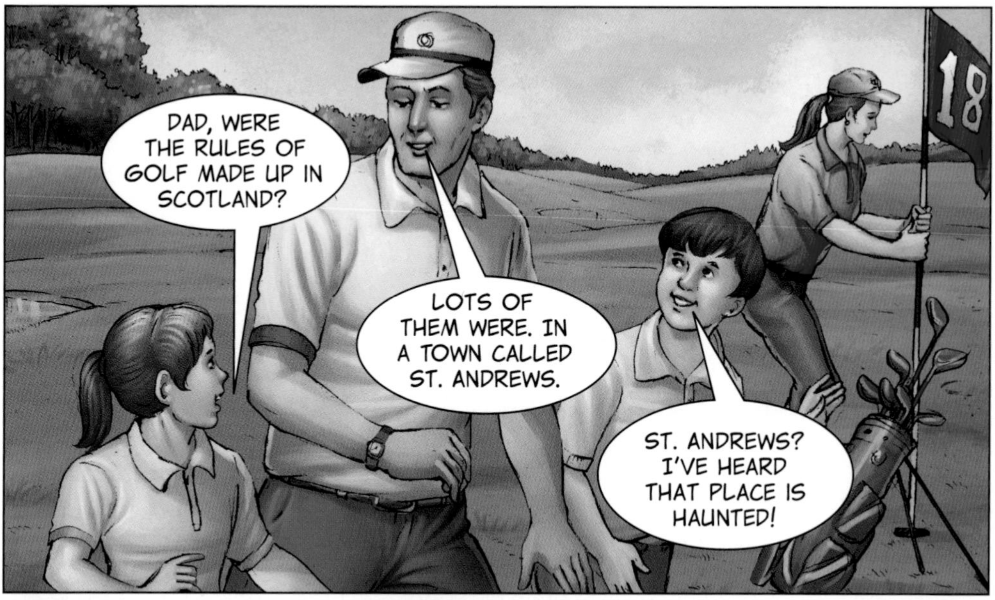
DAD, WERE THE RULES OF GOLF MADE UP IN SCOTLAND?
LOTS OF THEM WERE. IN A TOWN CALLED ST. ANDREWS.
ST. ANDREWS? I'VE HEARD THAT PLACE IS HAUNTED!
18

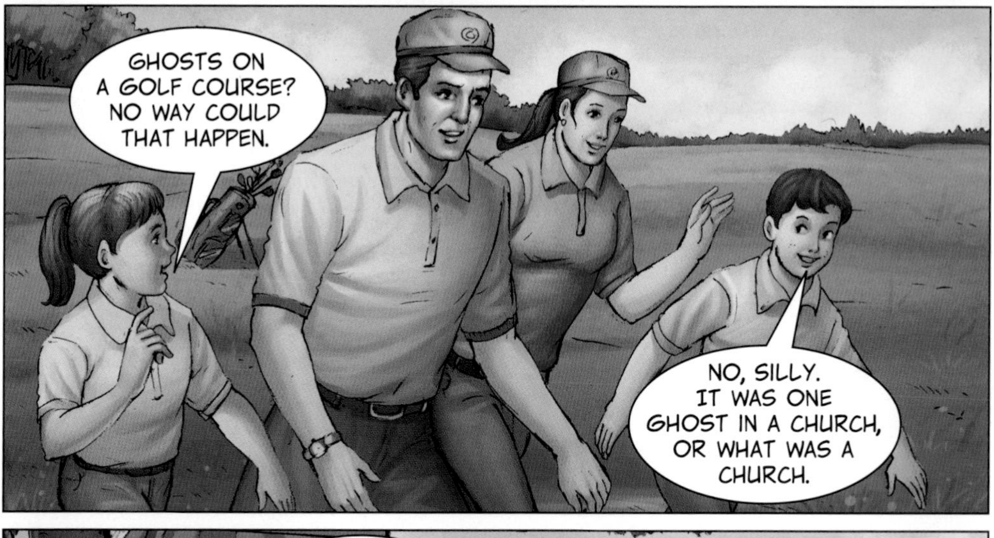
GHOSTS ON A GOLF COURSE? NO WAY COULD THAT HAPPEN.
NO, SILLY. IT WAS ONE GHOST IN A CHURCH, OR WHAT WAS A CHURCH.

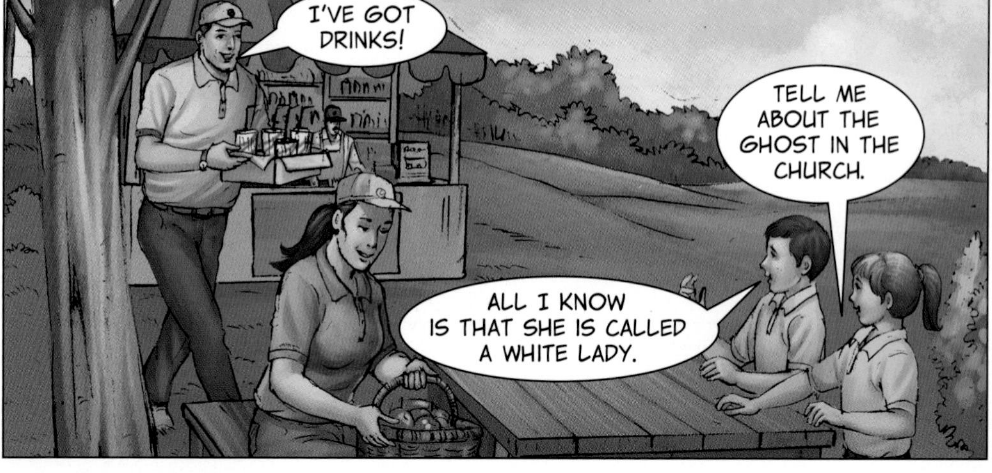
I'VE GOT DRINKS!
TELL ME ABOUT THE GHOST IN THE CHURCH.
ALL I KNOW IS THAT SHE IS CALLED A WHITE LADY.

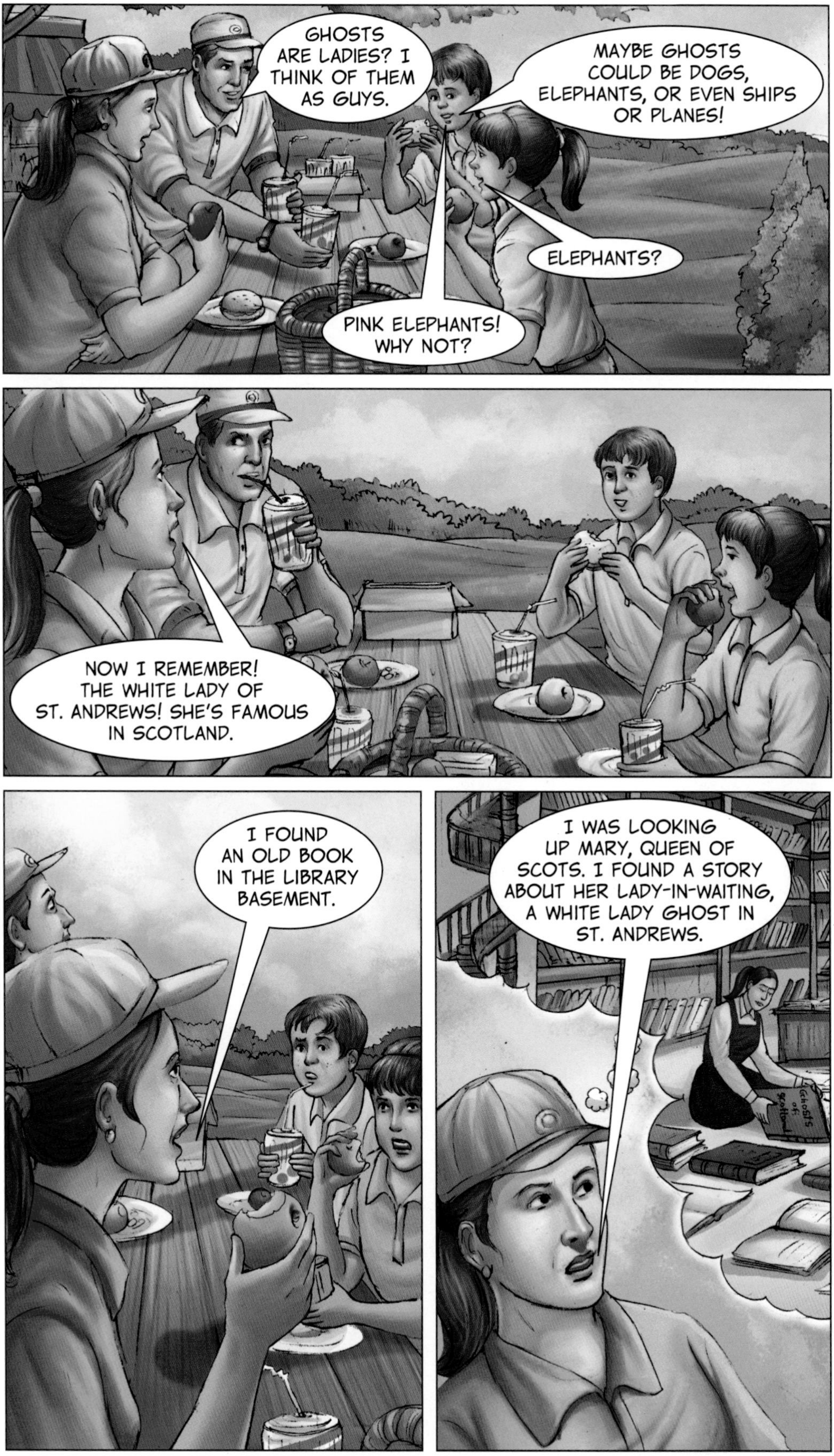
GHOSTS ARE LADIES? I THINK OF THEM AS GUYS.
MAYBE GHOSTS COULD BE DOGS, ELEPHANTS, OR EVEN SHIPS OR PLANES!
ELEPHANTS?
PINK ELEPHANTS! WHY NOT?
NOW I REMEMBER! THE WHITE LADY OF ST. ANDREWS! SHE'S FAMOUS IN SCOTLAND.
I FOUND AN OLD BOOK IN THE LIBRARY BASEMENT.
I WAS LOOKING UP MARY, QUEEN OF SCOTS. I FOUND A STORY ABOUT HER LADY-IN-WAITING, A WHITE LADY GHOST IN ST. ANDREWS.
GHOSTS of SCOTLAND

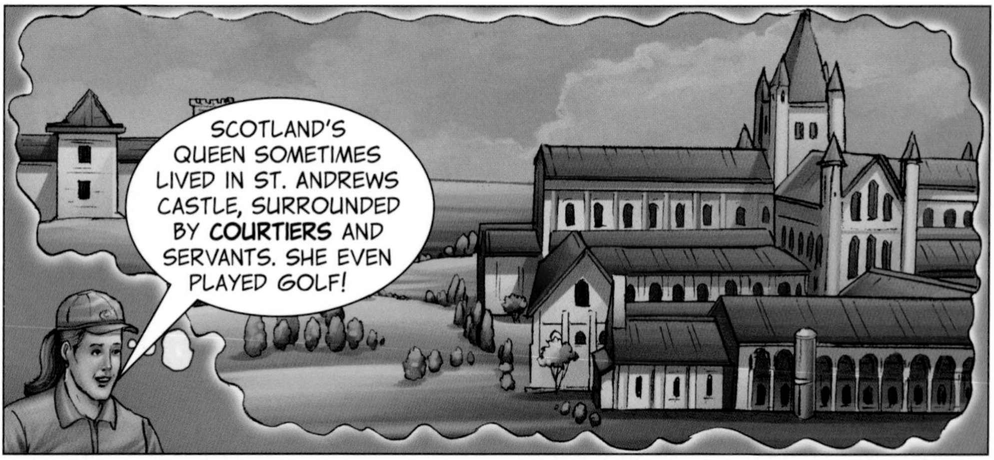
SCOTLAND'S QUEEN SOMETIMES LIVED IN ST. ANDREWS CASTLE, SURROUNDED BY **COURTIERS** AND SERVANTS. SHE EVEN PLAYED GOLF!

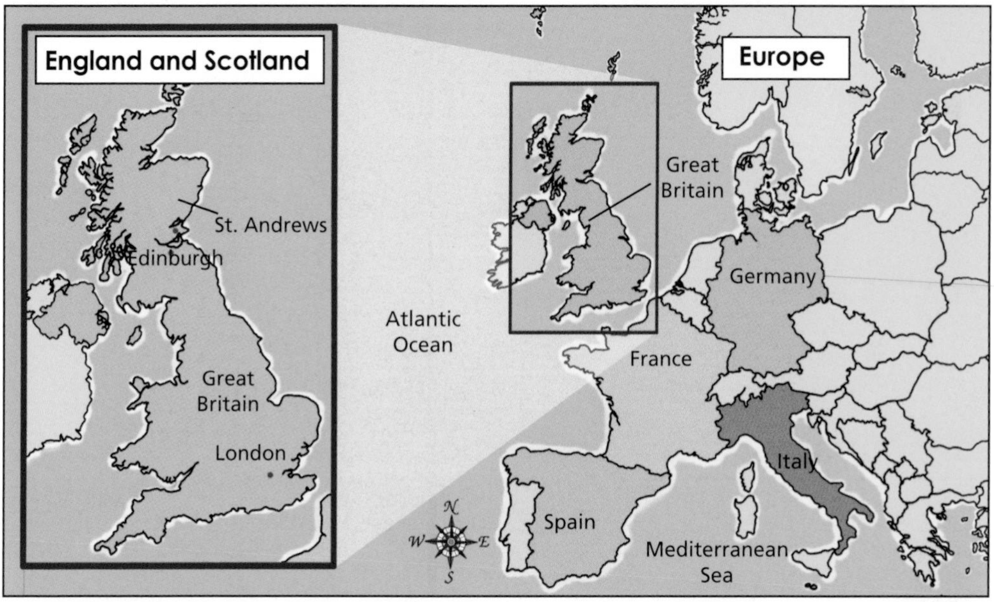
England and Scotland
St. Andrews
Edinburgh
Great Britain
London
Europe
Great Britain
Germany
Atlantic Ocean
France
Italy
Spain
N
W
E
S
Mediterranean Sea

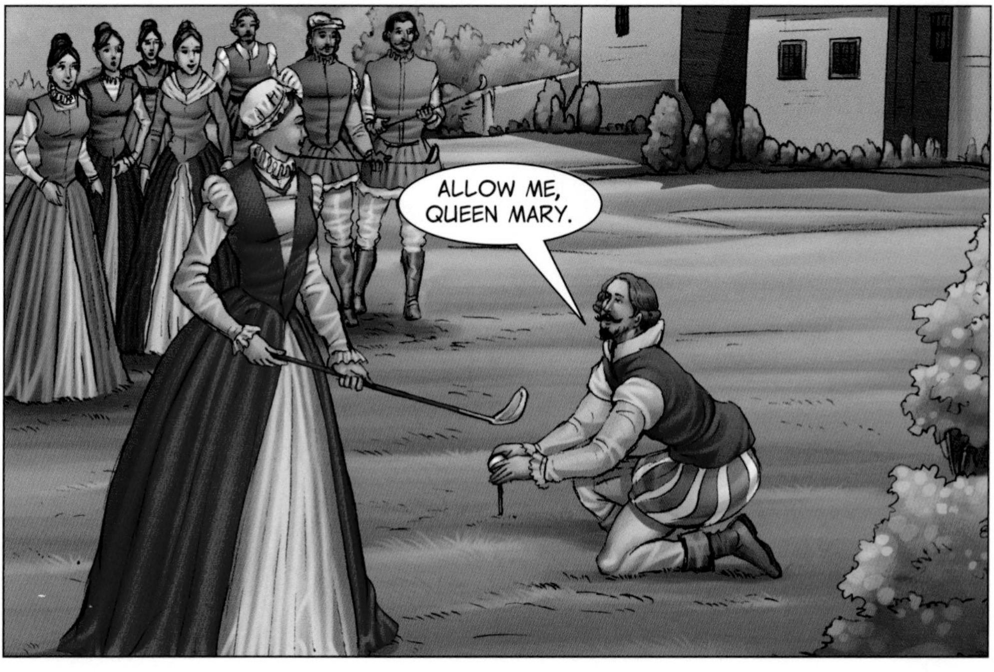
ALLOW ME, QUEEN MARY.

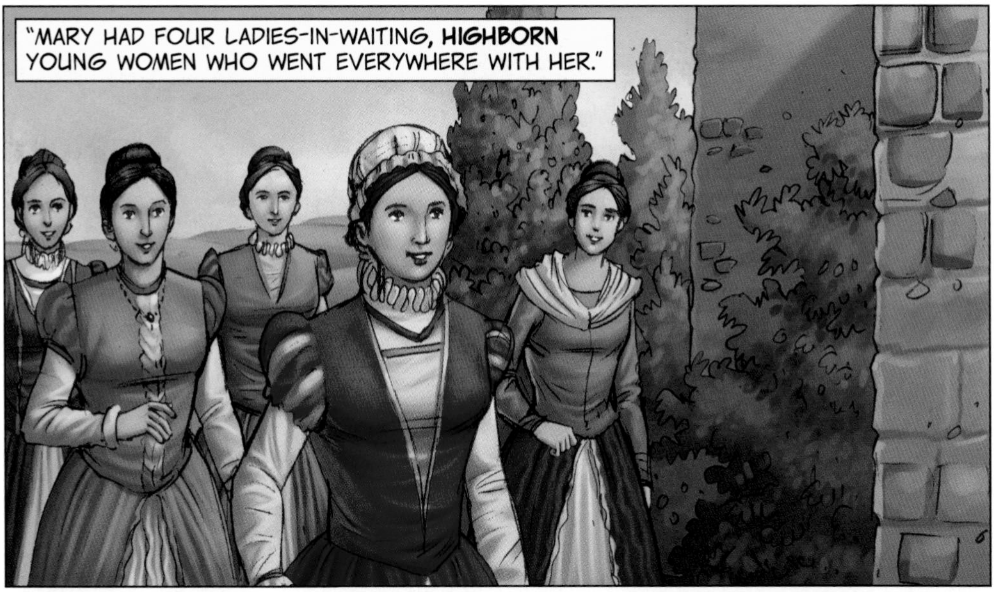
"MARY HAD FOUR LADIES-IN-WAITING, **HIGHBORN** YOUNG WOMEN WHO WENT EVERYWHERE WITH HER."

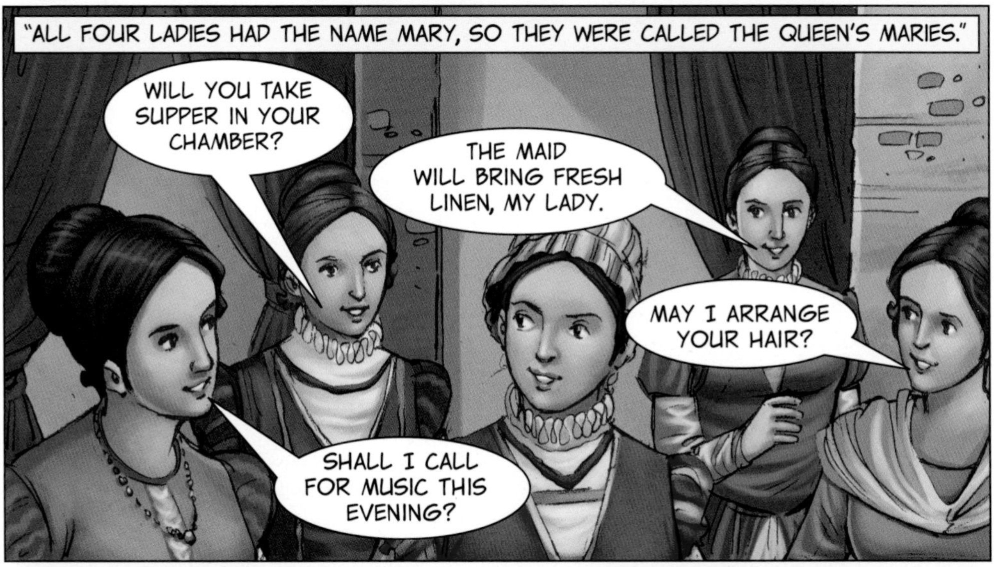
"ALL FOUR LADIES HAD THE NAME MARY, SO THEY WERE CALLED THE QUEEN'S MARIES."
WILL YOU TAKE SUPPER IN YOUR CHAMBER?
THE MAID WILL BRING FRESH LINEN, MY LADY.
MAY I ARRANGE YOUR HAIR?
SHALL I CALL FOR MUSIC THIS EVENING?

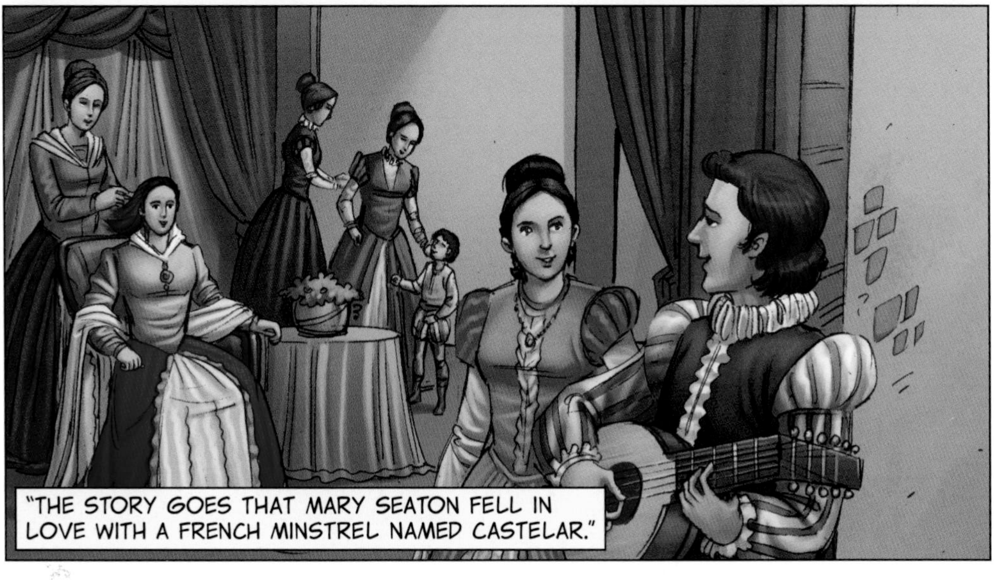
"THE STORY GOES THAT MARY SEATON FELL IN LOVE WITH A FRENCH MINSTREL NAMED CASTELAR."

"CASTELAR PLAYED LOVELY MUSIC AND SANG LIKE A BIRD. HE ENTERTAINED THE LORDS AND LADIES WITH SONGS AND POETRY."

"THE LADIES MAY HAVE ADORED CASTELAR, BUT HE MADE POWERFUL ENEMIES. HE WAS SENTENCED TO DEATH AND THROWN INTO THE CASTLE DUNGEON."

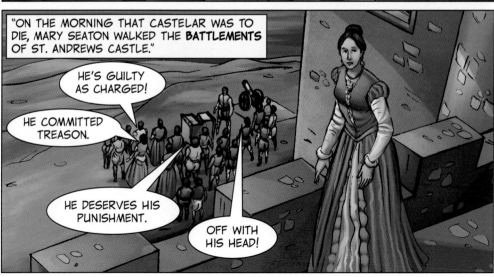

"ON THE MORNING THAT CASTELAR WAS TO DIE, MARY SEATON WALKED THE **BATTLEMENTS** OF ST. ANDREWS CASTLE."

HE'S GUILTY AS CHARGED!

HE COMMITTED TREASON.

HE DESERVES HIS PUNISHMENT.

OFF WITH HIS HEAD!

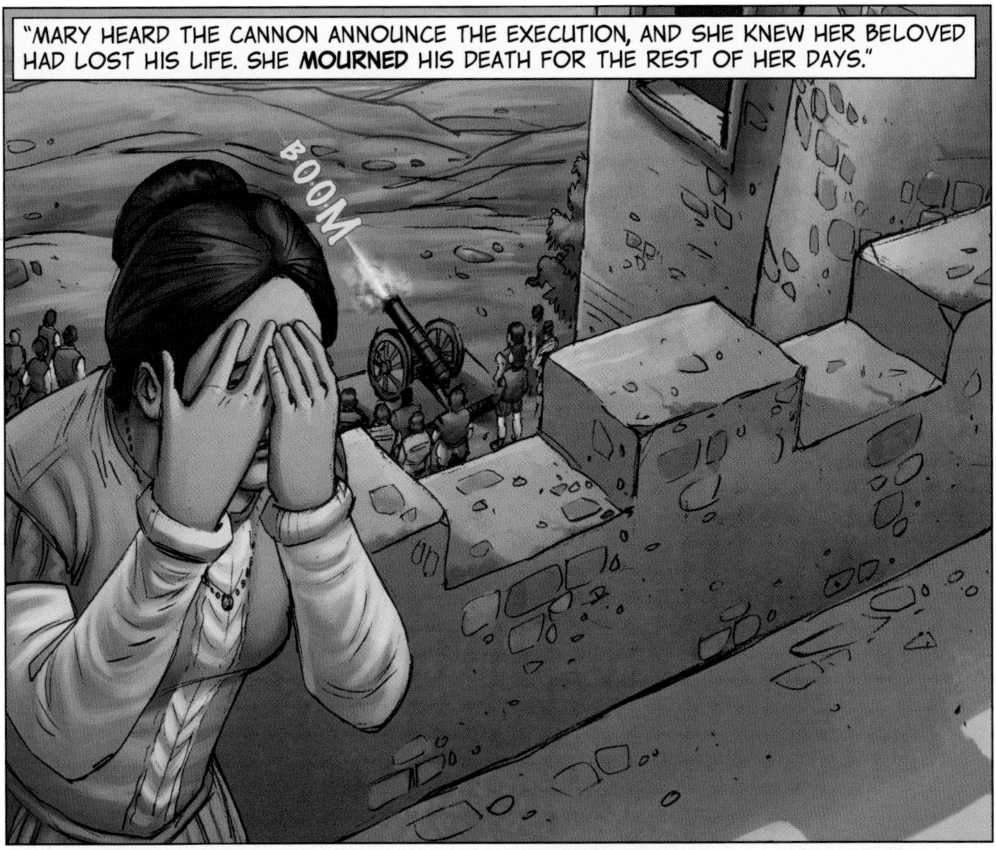
"MARY HEARD THE CANNON ANNOUNCE THE EXECUTION, AND SHE KNEW HER BELOVED HAD LOST HIS LIFE. SHE **MOURNED** HIS DEATH FOR THE REST OF HER DAYS."
BOOM

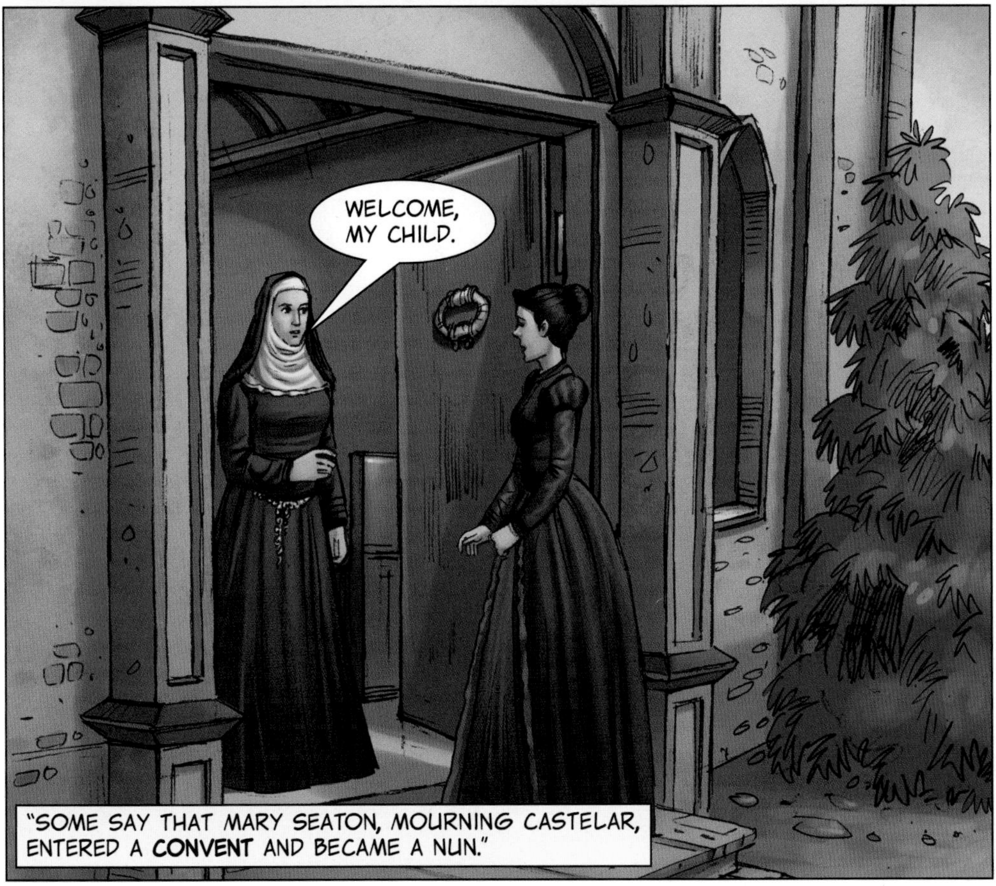
WELCOME, MY CHILD.
"SOME SAY THAT MARY SEATON, MOURNING CASTELAR, ENTERED A **CONVENT** AND BECAME A NUN."

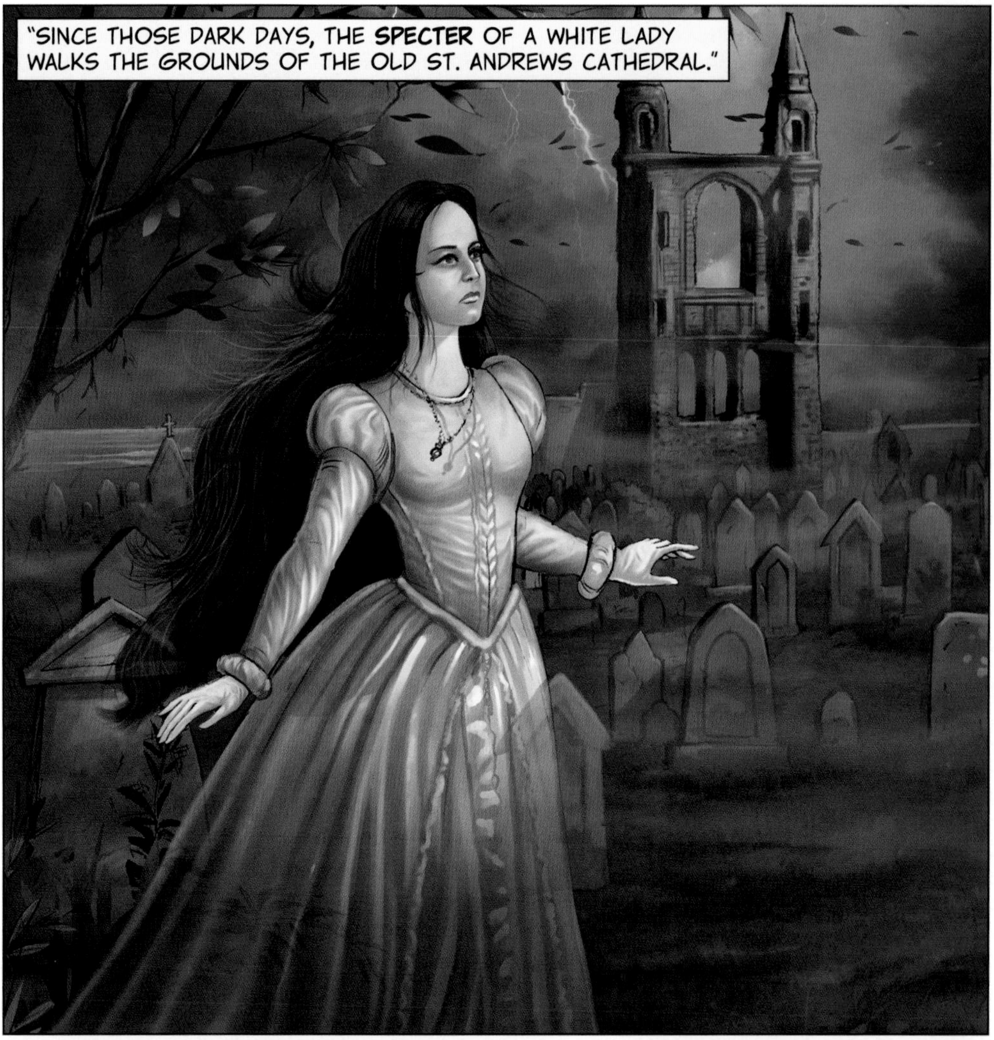
"SINCE THOSE DARK DAYS, THE **SPECTER** OF A WHITE LADY WALKS THE GROUNDS OF THE OLD ST. ANDREWS CATHEDRAL."

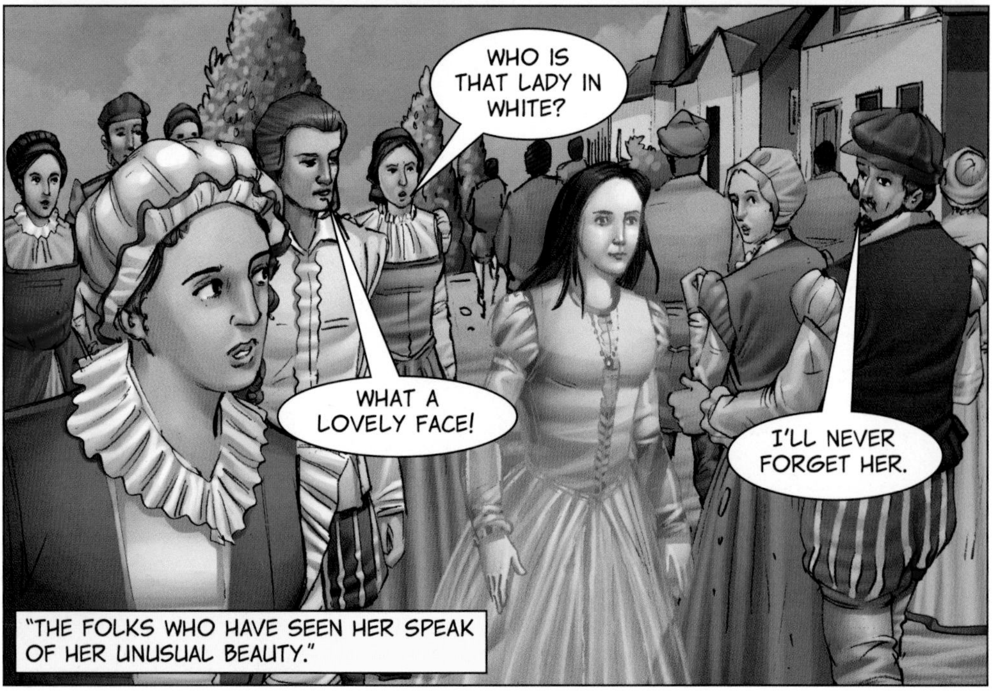
WHO IS THAT LADY IN WHITE?
WHAT A LOVELY FACE!
I'LL NEVER FORGET HER.
"THE FOLKS WHO HAVE SEEN HER SPEAK OF HER UNUSUAL BEAUTY."

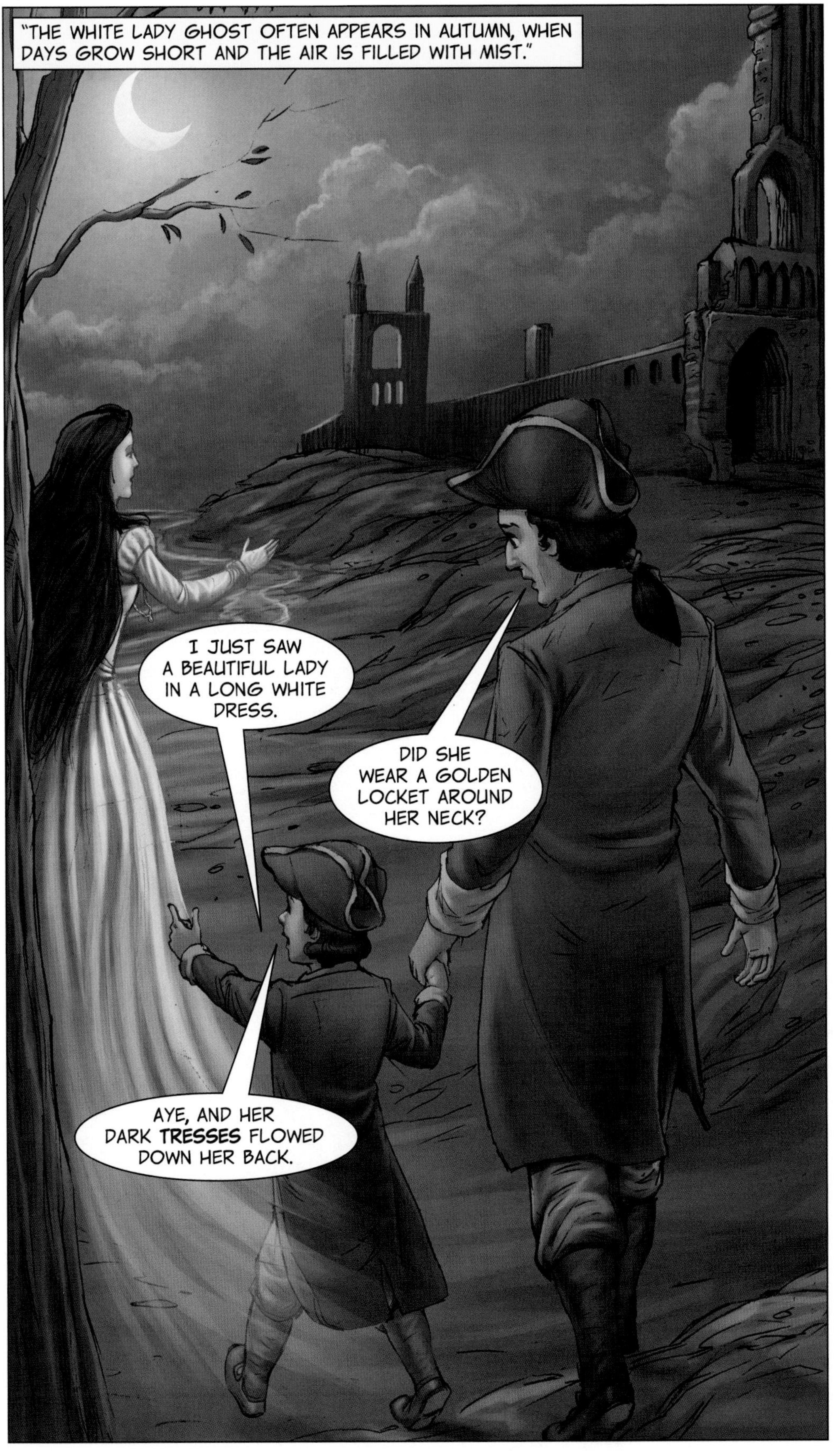
"THE WHITE LADY GHOST OFTEN APPEARS IN AUTUMN, WHEN DAYS GROW SHORT AND THE AIR IS FILLED WITH MIST."
I JUST SAW A BEAUTIFUL LADY IN A LONG WHITE DRESS.
DID SHE WEAR A GOLDEN LOCKET AROUND HER NECK?
AYE, AND HER DARK **TRESSES** FLOWED DOWN HER BACK.

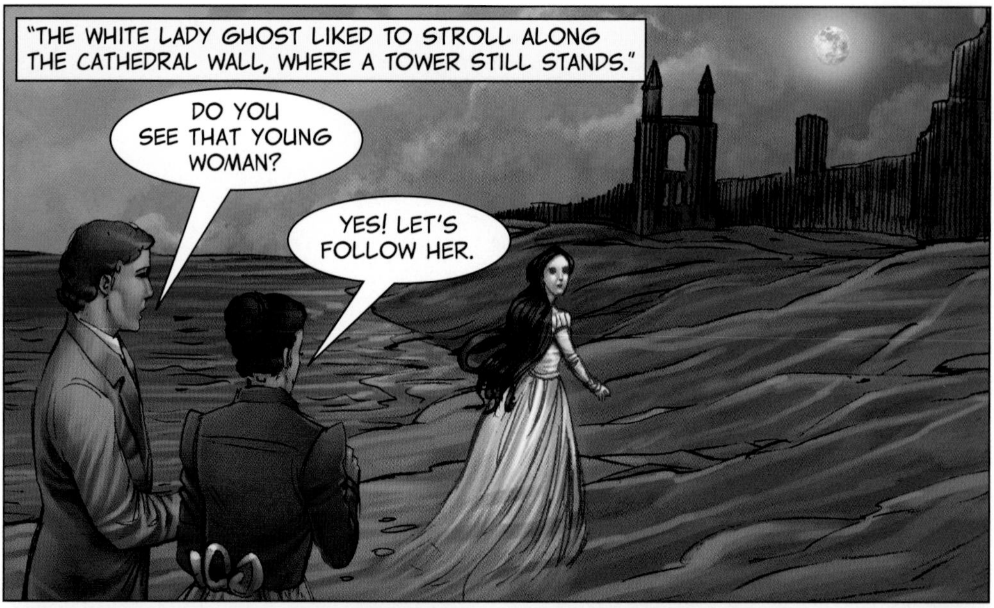
"THE WHITE LADY GHOST LIKED TO STROLL ALONG THE CATHEDRAL WALL, WHERE A TOWER STILL STANDS."
DO YOU SEE THAT YOUNG WOMAN?
YES! LET'S FOLLOW HER.

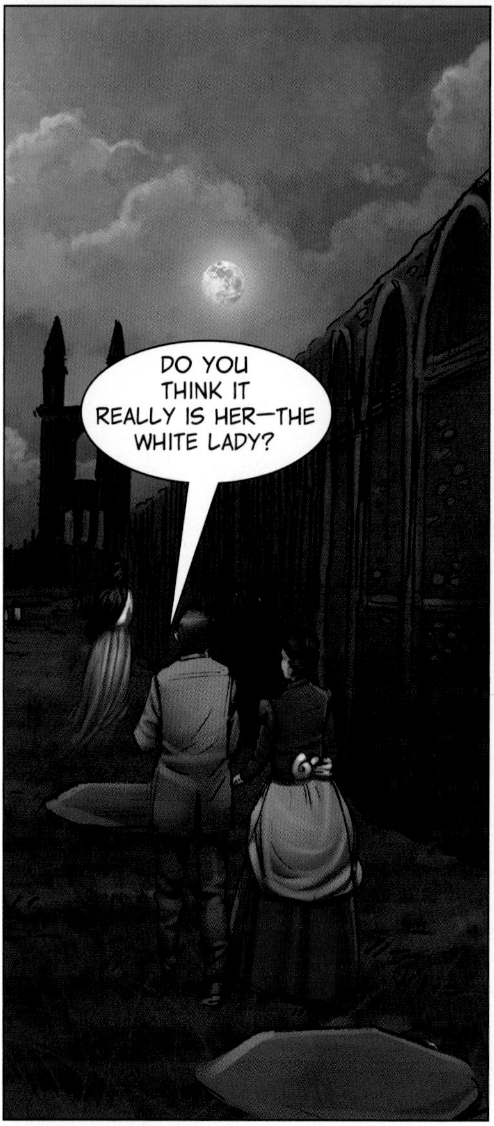
DO YOU THINK IT REALLY IS HER—THE WHITE LADY?

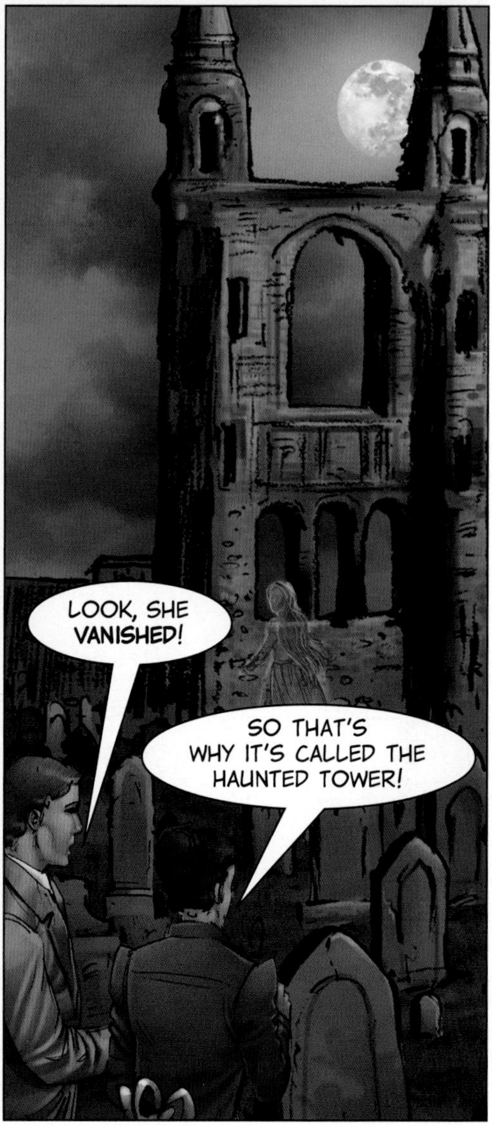
LOOK, SHE VANISHED!
SO THAT'S WHY IT'S CALLED THE HAUNTED TOWER!

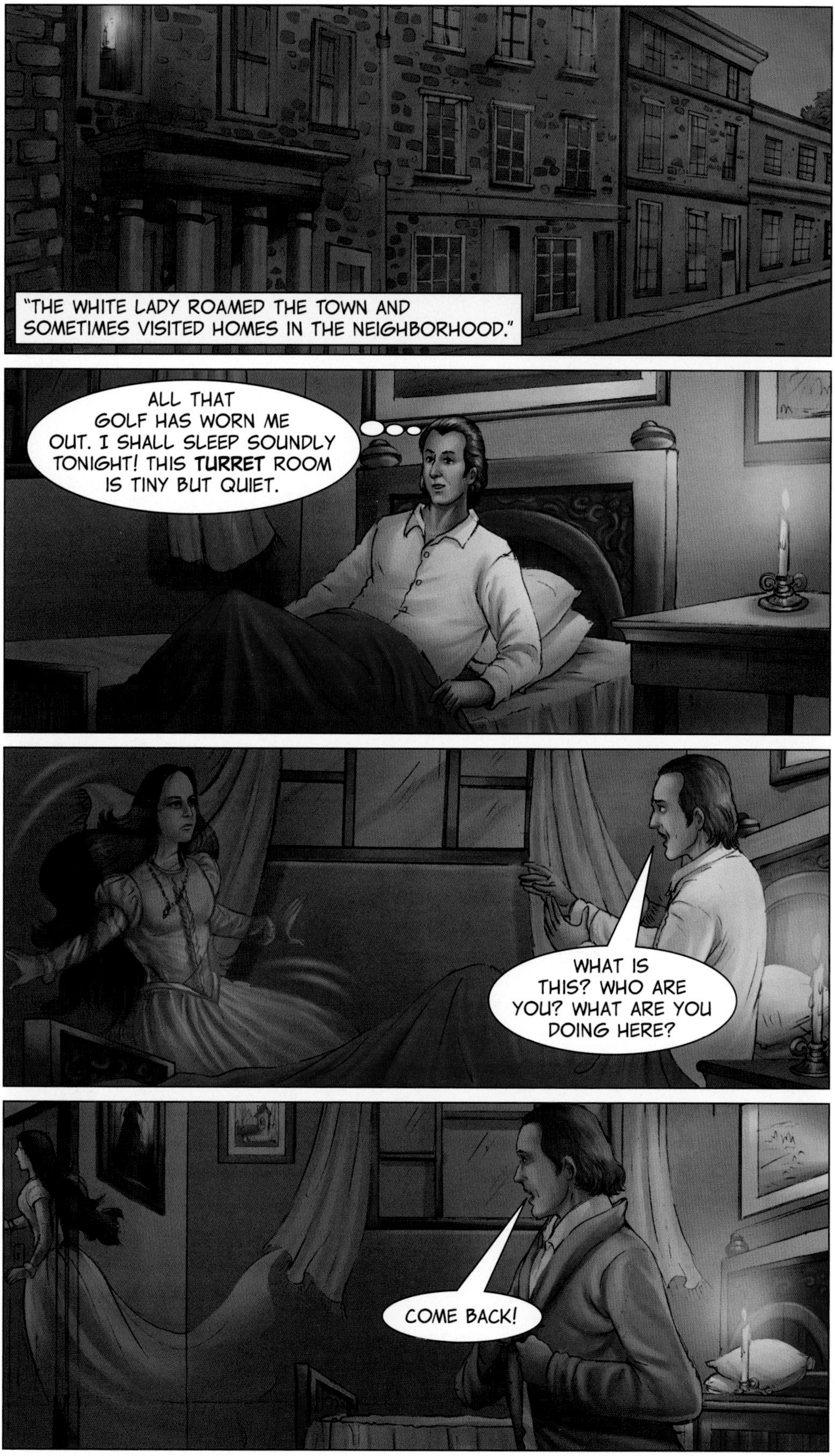
"THE WHITE LADY ROAMED THE TOWN AND SOMETIMES VISITED HOMES IN THE NEIGHBORHOOD."
ALL THAT GOLF HAS WORN ME OUT. I SHALL SLEEP SOUNDLY TONIGHT! THIS **TURRET** ROOM IS TINY BUT QUIET.
WHAT IS THIS? WHO ARE YOU? WHAT ARE YOU DOING HERE?
COME BACK!

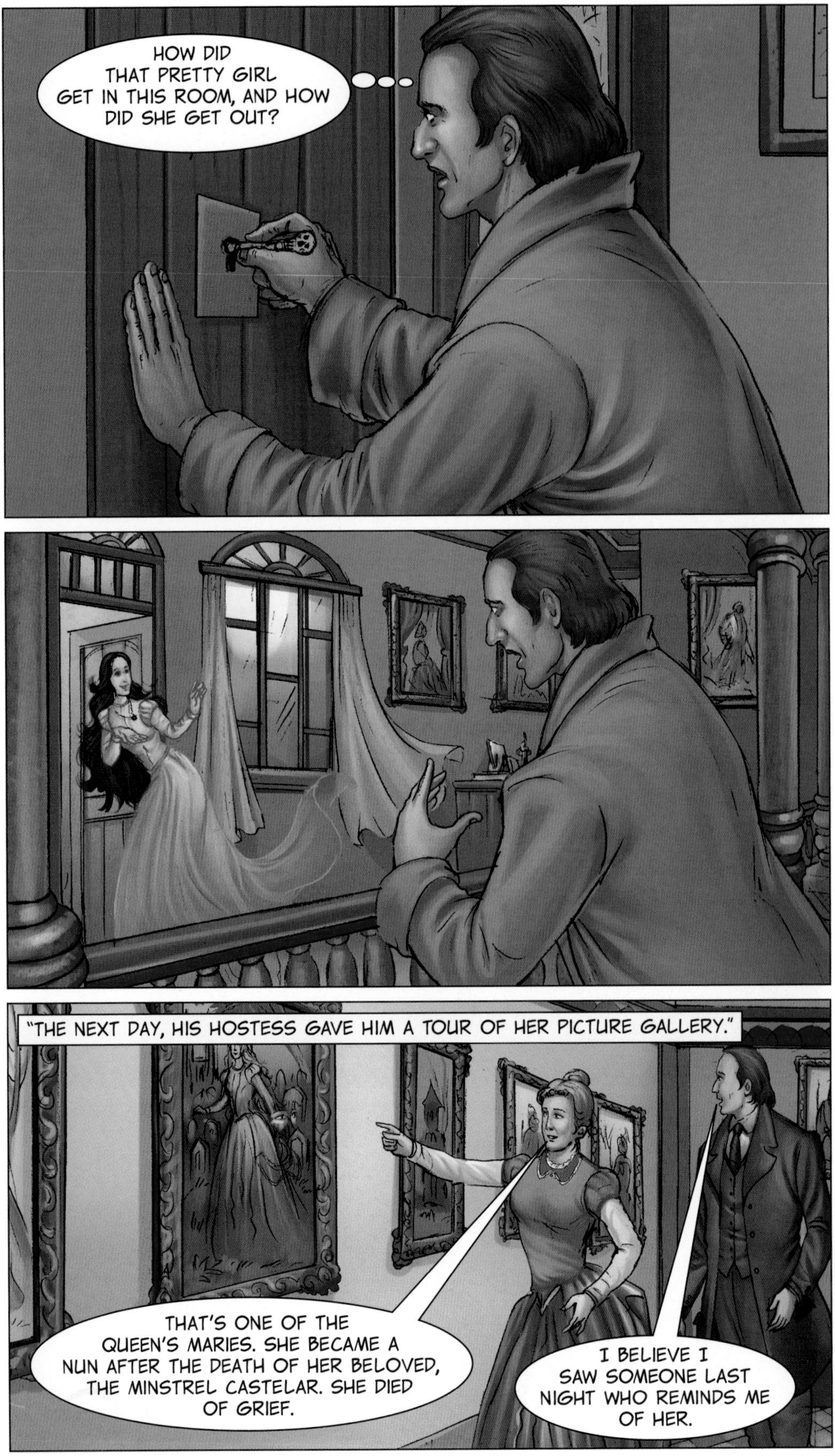
HOW DID THAT PRETTY GIRL GET IN THIS ROOM, AND HOW DID SHE GET OUT?
"THE NEXT DAY, HIS HOSTESS GAVE HIM A TOUR OF HER PICTURE GALLERY."
THAT'S ONE OF THE QUEEN'S MARIES. SHE BECAME A NUN AFTER THE DEATH OF HER BELOVED, THE MINSTREL CASTELAR. SHE DIED OF GRIEF.
I BELIEVE I SAW SOMEONE LAST NIGHT WHO REMINDS ME OF HER.

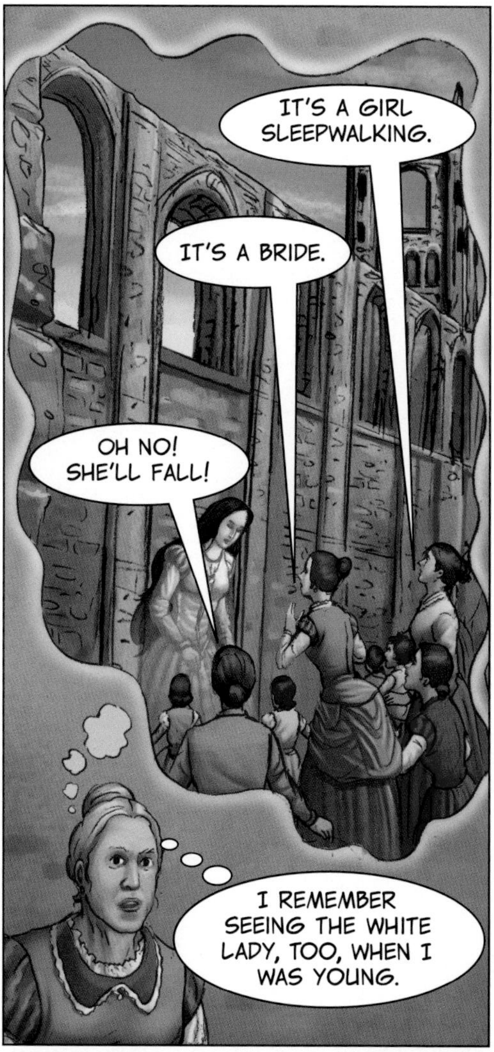
IT'S A GIRL SLEEPWALKING.
IT'S A BRIDE.
OH NO! SHE'LL FALL!
I REMEMBER SEEING THE WHITE LADY, TOO, WHEN I WAS YOUNG.

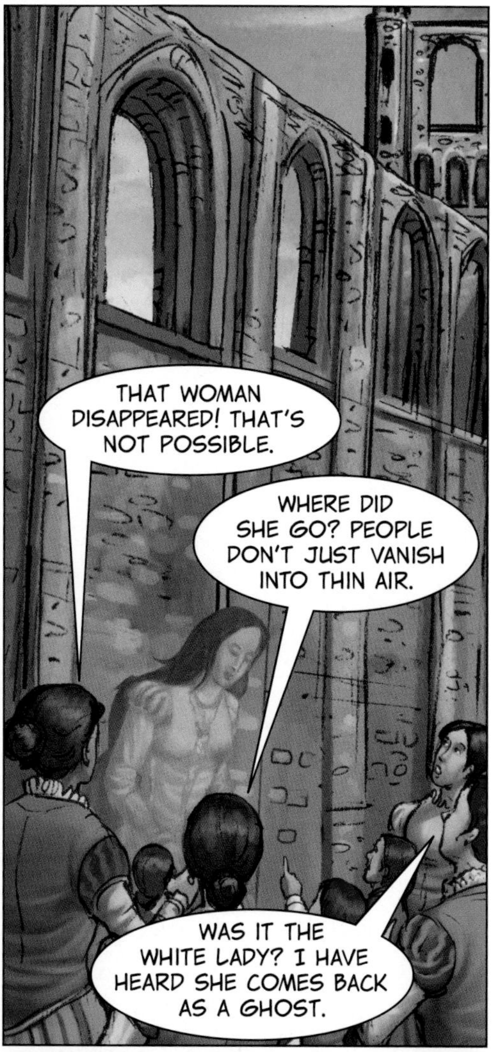
THAT WOMAN DISAPPEARED! THAT'S NOT POSSIBLE.
WHERE DID SHE GO? PEOPLE DON'T JUST VANISH INTO THIN AIR.
WAS IT THE WHITE LADY? I HAVE HEARD SHE COMES BACK AS A GHOST.

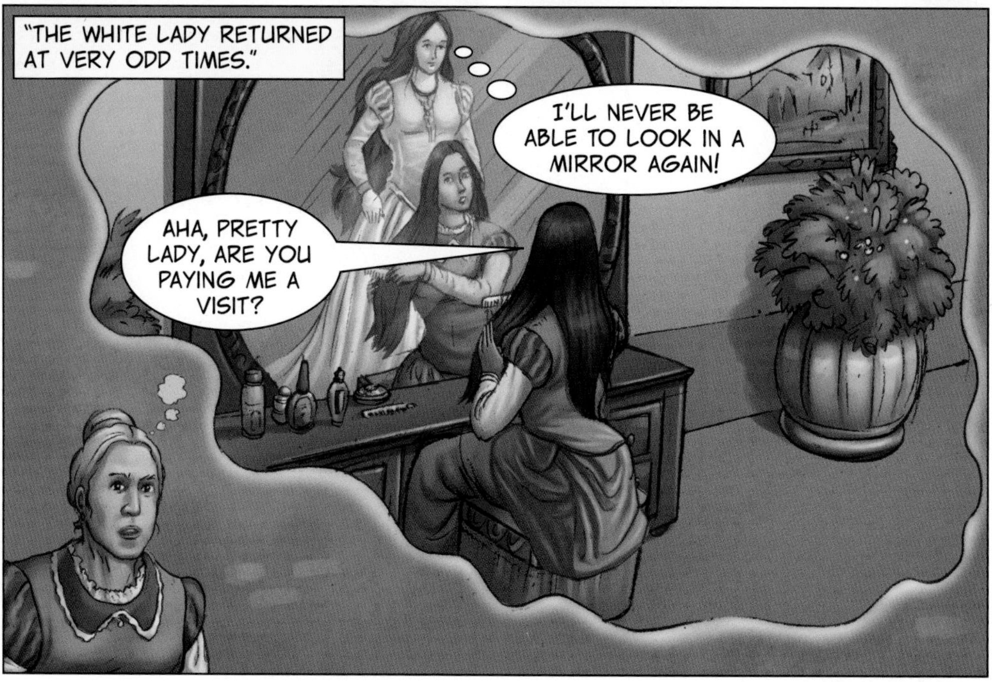
"THE WHITE LADY RETURNED AT VERY ODD TIMES."
I'LL NEVER BE ABLE TO LOOK IN A MIRROR AGAIN!
AHA, PRETTY LADY, ARE YOU PAYING ME A VISIT?

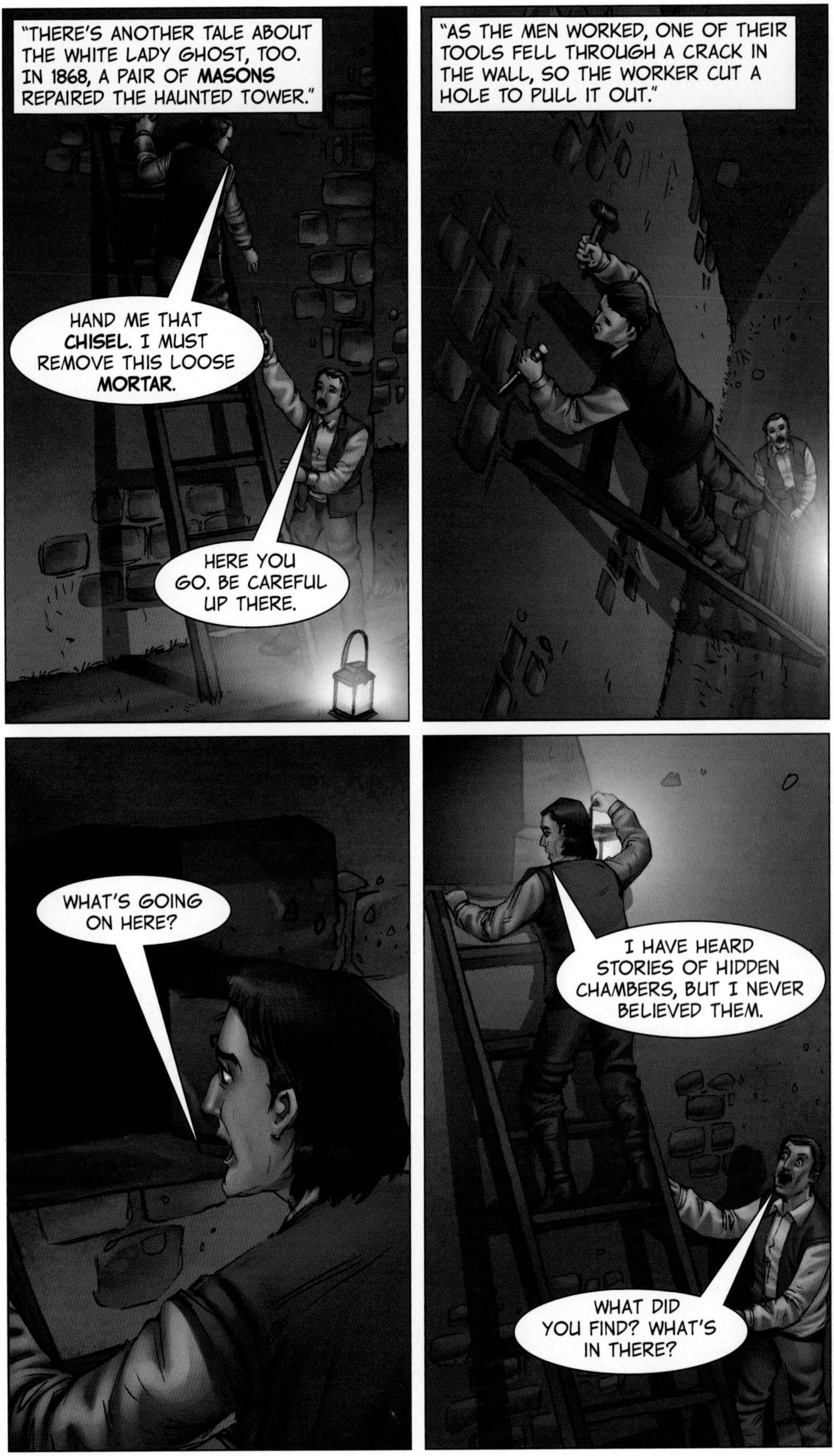
"THERE'S ANOTHER TALE ABOUT THE WHITE LADY GHOST, TOO. IN 1868, A PAIR OF MASONS REPAIRED THE HAUNTED TOWER."
HAND ME THAT CHISEL. I MUST REMOVE THIS LOOSE MORTAR.
HERE YOU GO. BE CAREFUL UP THERE.
"AS THE MEN WORKED, ONE OF THEIR TOOLS FELL THROUGH A CRACK IN THE WALL, SO THE WORKER CUT A HOLE TO PULL IT OUT."
WHAT'S GOING ON HERE?
I HAVE HEARD STORIES OF HIDDEN CHAMBERS, BUT I NEVER BELIEVED THEM.
WHAT DID YOU FIND? WHAT'S IN THERE?

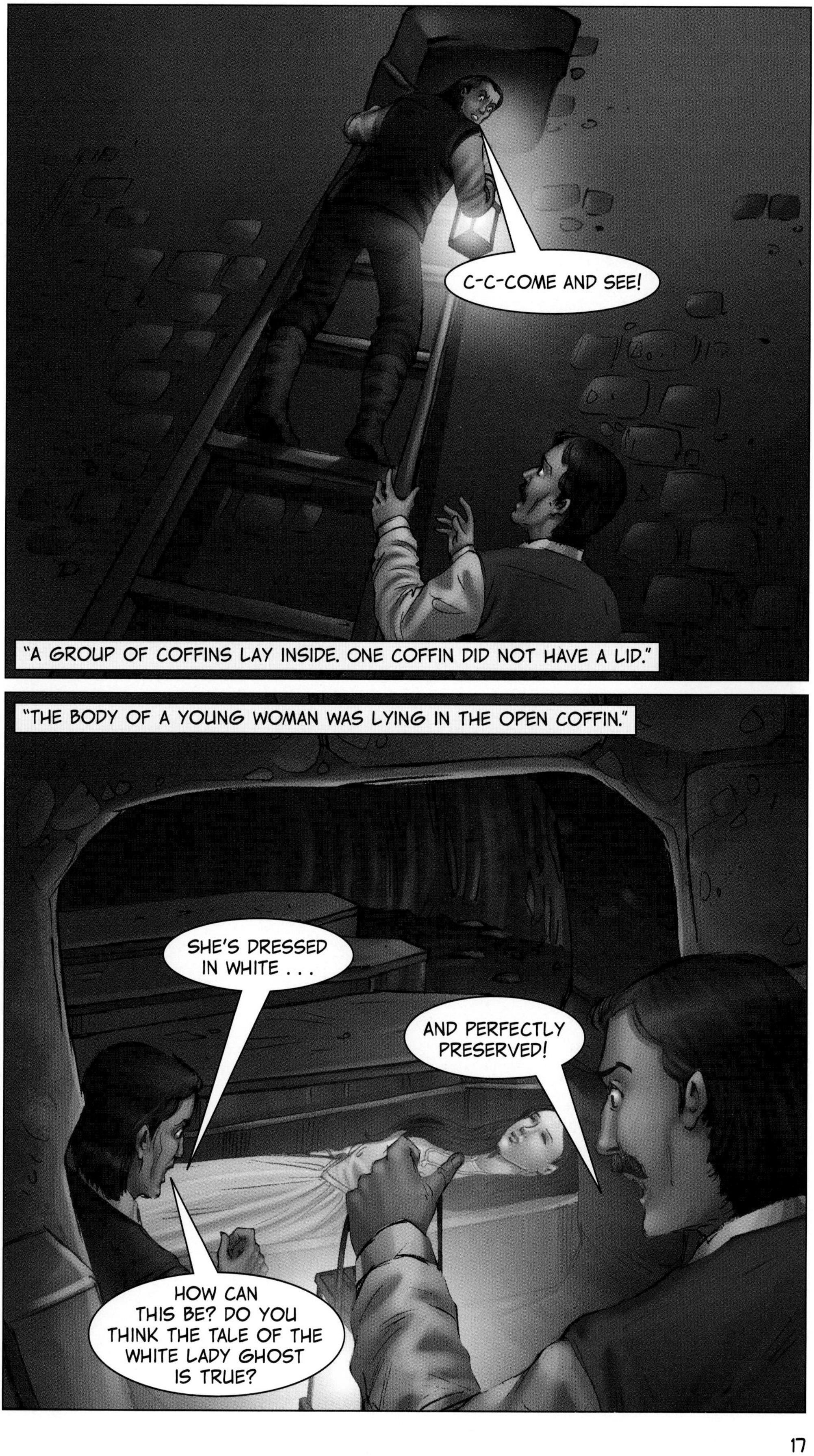
C-C-COME AND SEE!
"A GROUP OF COFFINS LAY INSIDE. ONE COFFIN DID NOT HAVE A LID."
"THE BODY OF A YOUNG WOMAN WAS LYING IN THE OPEN COFFIN."
SHE'S DRESSED IN WHITE . . .
AND PERFECTLY PRESERVED!
HOW CAN THIS BE? DO YOU THINK THE TALE OF THE WHITE LADY GHOST IS TRUE?

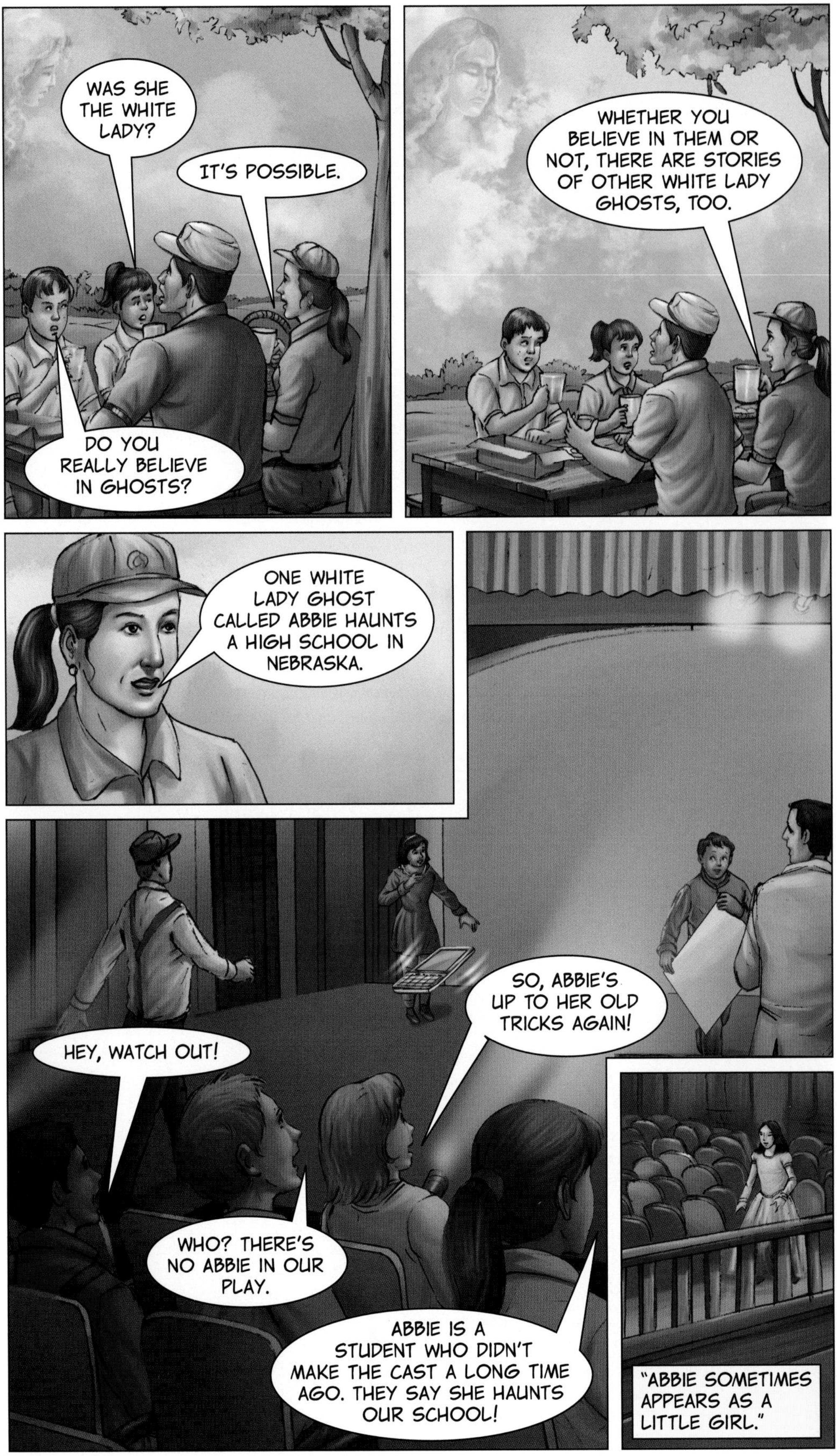
WAS SHE THE WHITE LADY?
IT'S POSSIBLE.
DO YOU REALLY BELIEVE IN GHOSTS?
WHETHER YOU BELIEVE IN THEM OR NOT, THERE ARE STORIES OF OTHER WHITE LADY GHOSTS, TOO.
ONE WHITE LADY GHOST CALLED ABBIE HAUNTS A HIGH SCHOOL IN NEBRASKA.
HEY, WATCH OUT!
SO, ABBIE'S UP TO HER OLD TRICKS AGAIN!
WHO? THERE'S NO ABBIE IN OUR PLAY.
ABBIE IS A STUDENT WHO DIDN'T MAKE THE CAST A LONG TIME AGO. THEY SAY SHE HAUNTS OUR SCHOOL!
"ABBIE SOMETIMES APPEARS AS A LITTLE GIRL."

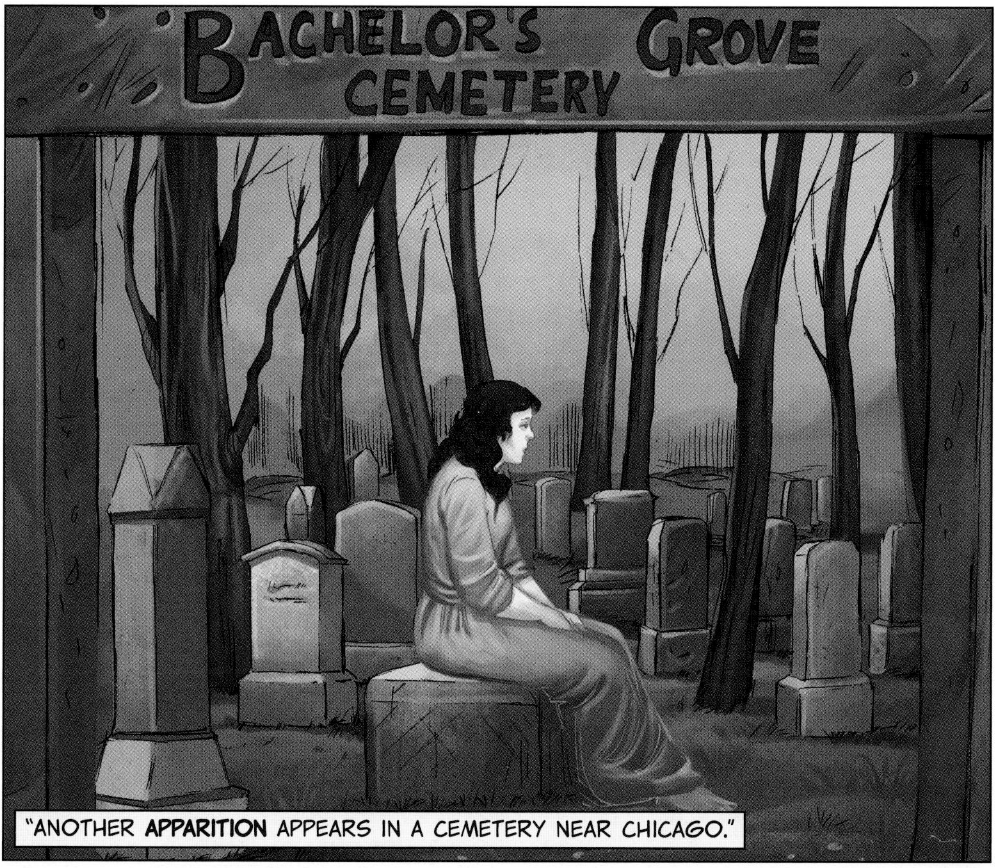
BACHELOR'S GROVE CEMETERY
"ANOTHER APPARITION APPEARS IN A CEMETERY NEAR CHICAGO."

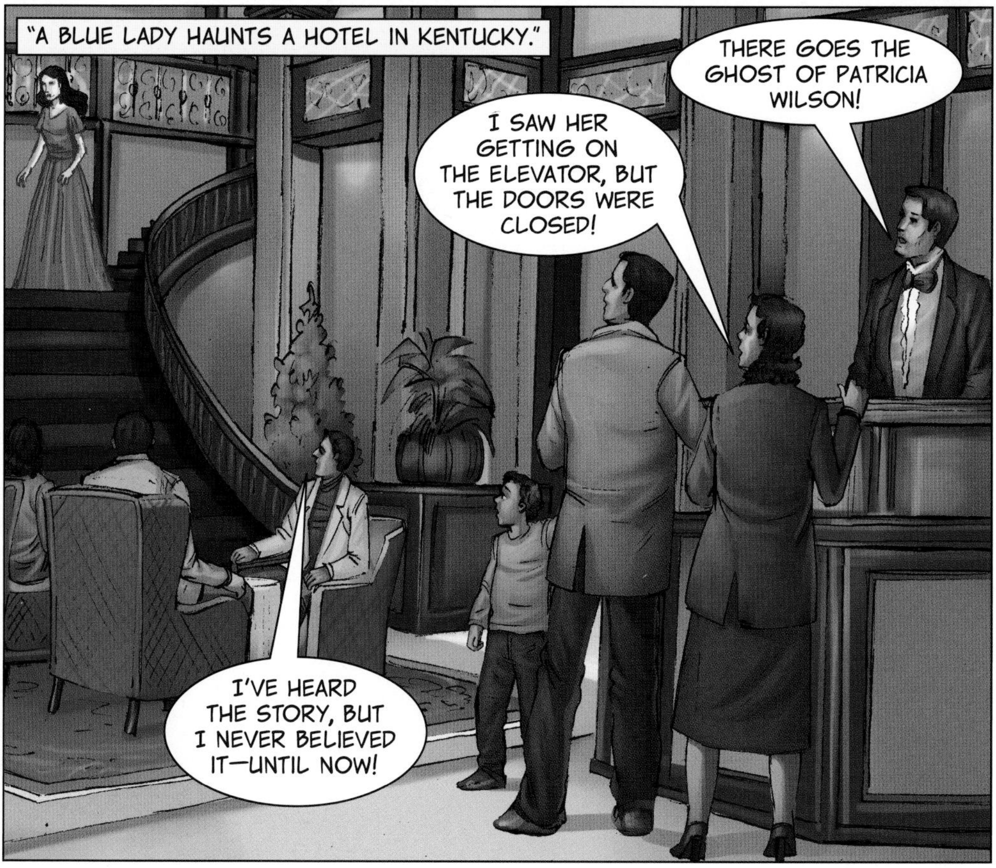
"A BLUE LADY HAUNTS A HOTEL IN KENTUCKY."
THERE GOES THE GHOST OF PATRICIA WILSON!
I SAW HER GETTING ON THE ELEVATOR, BUT THE DOORS WERE CLOSED!
I'VE HEARD THE STORY, BUT I NEVER BELIEVED IT—UNTIL NOW!

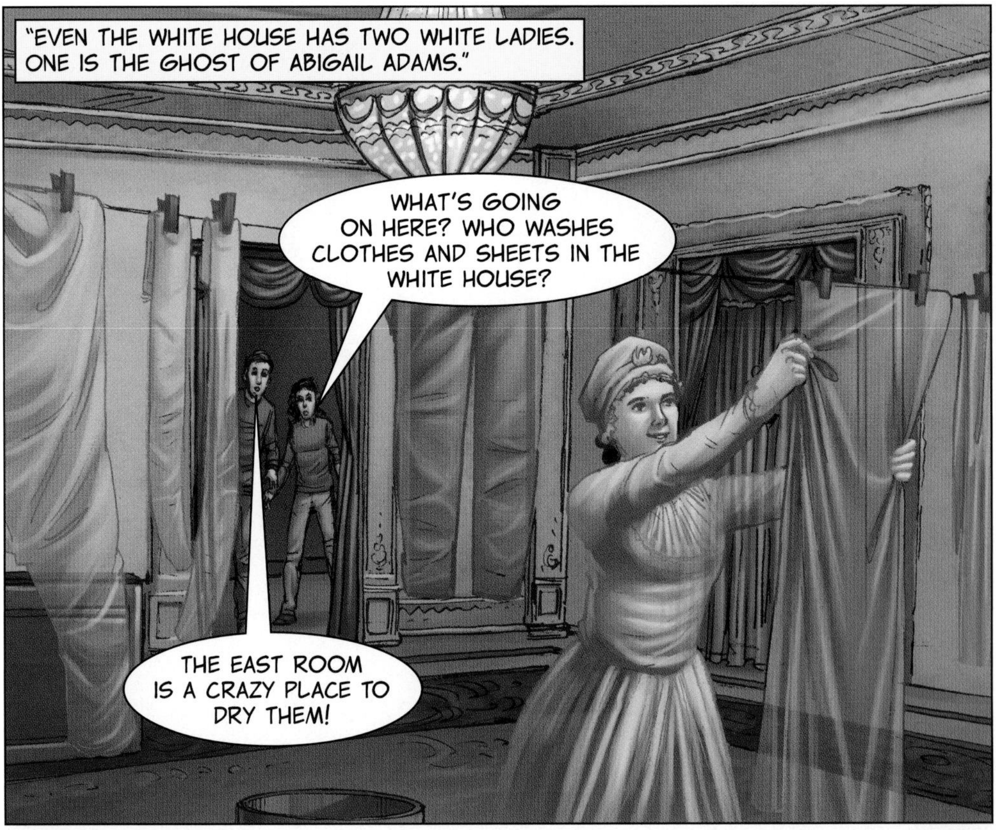
"EVEN THE WHITE HOUSE HAS TWO WHITE LADIES. ONE IS THE GHOST OF ABIGAIL ADAMS."
WHAT'S GOING ON HERE? WHO WASHES CLOTHES AND SHEETS IN THE WHITE HOUSE?
THE EAST ROOM IS A CRAZY PLACE TO DRY THEM!

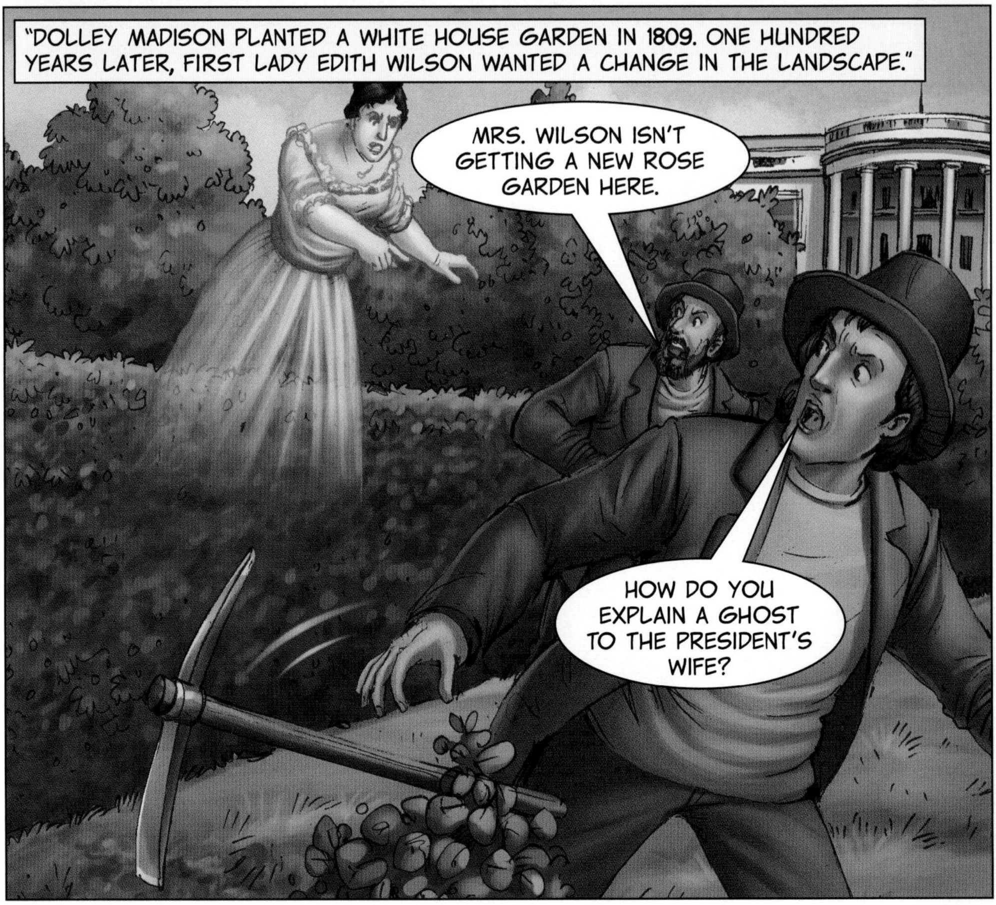
"DOLLEY MADISON PLANTED A WHITE HOUSE GARDEN IN 1809. ONE HUNDRED YEARS LATER, FIRST LADY EDITH WILSON WANTED A CHANGE IN THE LANDSCAPE."
MRS. WILSON ISN'T GETTING A NEW ROSE GARDEN HERE.
HOW DO YOU EXPLAIN A GHOST TO THE PRESIDENT'S WIFE?

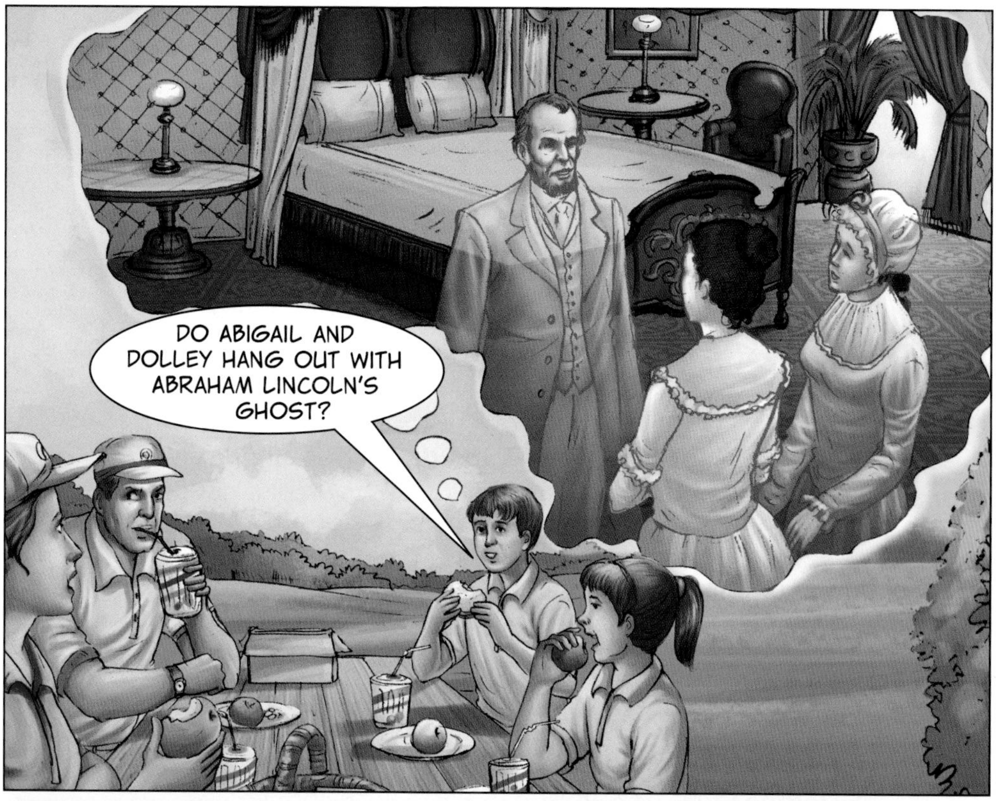
DO ABIGAIL AND DOLLEY HANG OUT WITH ABRAHAM LINCOLN'S GHOST?

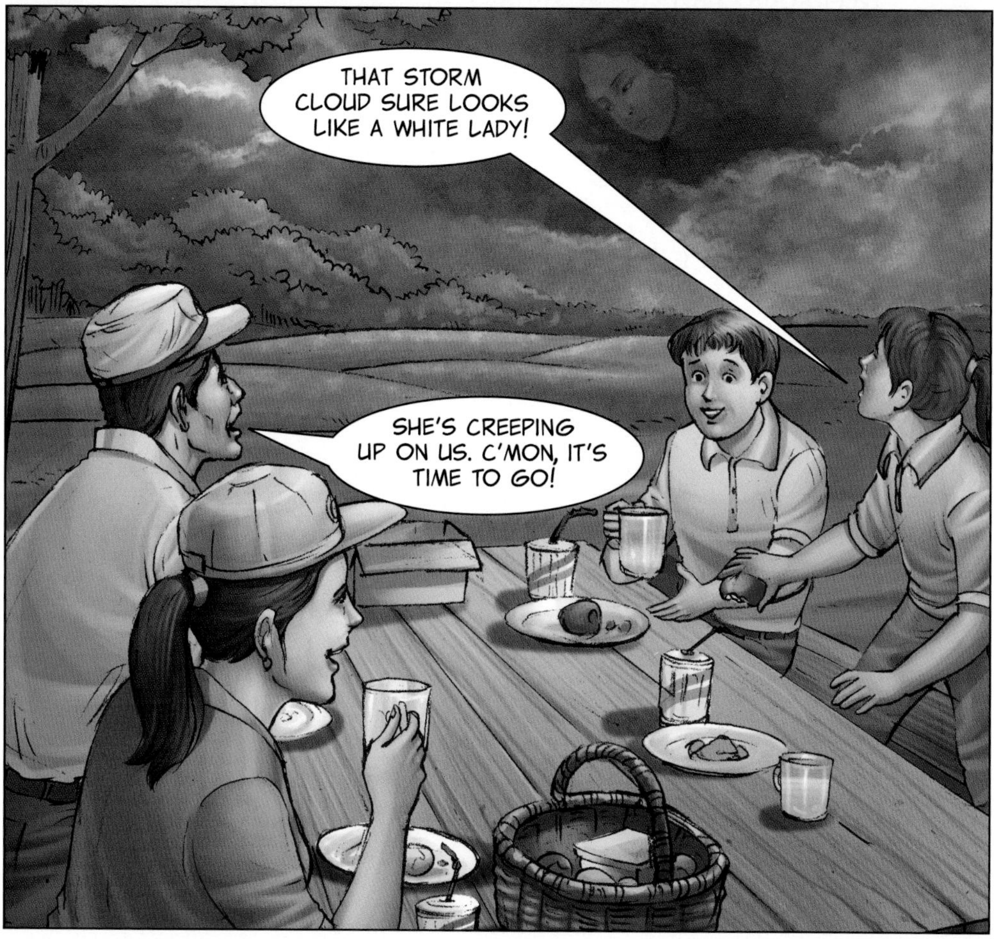
THAT STORM CLOUD SURE LOOKS LIKE A WHITE LADY!
SHE'S CREEPING UP ON US. C'MON, IT'S TIME TO GO!

Index

Websites

Due to the changing nature of Internet links, PowerKids Press has developed an online list of websites related to the subject of this book. This site is updated regularly. Please use this link to access the list:

www.powerkidslinks.com/jggs/lady/